W9-ACG-638

We
Shall
Overcome

The Little Rock Nine

Rachel Tisdale

PowerKiDS press.

New York

Published in 2014 by The Rosen Publishing Group
29 East 21st Street, New York, NY 10010

Produced for Rosen by Calcium Creative Ltd
Editor for Calcium Creative Ltd: Sarah Eason
US Editor: Joshua Shadowens
Designer: Paul Myerscough

Photo credits: Cover: Arkansas Dept of Parks and Tourism (bg), Corbis/Bettmann (fg).
Inside: Arkansas Department of Parks and Tourism: 3, 27, 28; Corbis: Bettmann 10, 13,
18; Library of Congress: World Telegram/Walter Albertin 1, 19, John T. Bledsoe 22, 23,
Jack Delano, FSA/OWI 6, Carol M. Highsmith Archive 12, Dorothea Lange, FSA/OWI 4,
Cecil Layne 9, Warren K. Leffler 26, Thomas J. O'Halloran 11, 17, Sun/Al Ravenna 7, Ben
Shahn, FSA/OWI 5, Marion S. Trikosko 14; National Civil Rights Museum: 25; Shutterstock:
Maximus256 8, Christopher Parypa 29; Wikimedia Commons: Brian Stansberry 21, US
Army 15, USIA photo 24.

Library of Congress Cataloging-in-Publication Data

Tisdale, Rachel.
 The Little Rock Nine / by Rachel Tisdale.
     pages cm. — (We shall overcome)
 Includes index.
 ISBN 978-1-4777-6057-4 (library) — ISBN 978-1-4777-6058-1 (pbk.) —
 ISBN 978-1-4777-6059-8 (6-pack)
 1. School integration—Arkansas—Little Rock—History—20th century—Juvenile literature.
 2. African American students—Arkansas—Little Rock—History—20th century—Juvenile
 literature. 3. Central High School (Little Rock, Ark.)—History—Juvenile literature. 4. Little
 Rock (Ark.)—Race relations—Juvenile literature. I. Title.
 LC214.23.L56T57 2014
 379.26309767'73—dc23
                                        2013024405

Manufactured in the United States of America

CPSIA Compliance Information: Batch #W14PK5: For Further Information contact Rosen Publishing, New York, New York at 1-800-237-9932

Contents

The Slavery Story

Today, all African Americans in the United States are free to vote, find paid work, and live wherever they choose. However, life for African Americans in the United States was once very different. Between 1619 and 1807, thousands of people were captured in Africa and transported to America. There, they were sold as slaves. These slaves were the first African Americans.

Slaves were put to work on farms called plantations, in factories, and in homes that belonged to white Americans.

Ending Slavery

In 1863, President Abraham Lincoln banned slavery. However, southern states soon found ways to limit the rights of African Americans by introducing laws that became known as the Jim Crow laws.

Segregation limited education for African American children.

Introducing Segregation

Jim Crow laws forced African Americans to be educated separately from white Americans, sit in separate areas in restaurants and on public transport, and even drink out of separate drinking fountains. These laws of separation became known as segregation. To challenge the rules of separation, African Americans formed a protest group called the National Association for the Advancement of Colored People (NAACP).

Fight for Rights

The NAACP was formed in 1909. The goal of the organization was to bring about an end to racial discrimination in the United States and to ensure that African Americans had the same civil rights as white Americans.

Education for All

To tackle the unfair system of education in the United States, the NAACP spent years gathering information about segregation in American schools. In the early 1950s, five cases made it to the US Supreme Court and together became known as the *Brown v. Board of Education* case. The case would change American history.

Many African American schools, like this one in Greene County, Georgia, had little money for new books and equipment.

An Unfair System

The *Brown v. Board of Education* case argued that the segregation laws in American schools were clearly unfair. White students traveled to school by bus, while African American children were made to walk to school, sometimes across large distances. Each year in South Carolina, an average of $179 per white American child was spent on education equipment, such as books. Just $43 per African American child was spent.

Righting the Wrong

The injustice toward African American children was plain to see and, in 1954, the US Supreme Court ruled that denying an African American child to attend an all-white school was wrong.

"Does segregation of children in public schools solely on the basis of race… deprive the children of the minority group of equal educational opportunities? We believe that it does."
US Supreme Court in *Brown v. Board of Education* case.

The *Brown v. Board of Education* case meant that African American children could now get an equal education, and go to school with white children. Linda Brown Smith (seen here on the left) was one of the children in the case.

No More Segregation?

Some people believed that the *Brown v. Board of Education* case would bring about an end to segregation in schools. However, the US Supreme Court ordered that segregation in schools was to be ended with "all deliberate speed." This meant that there was no date by which schools had to end segregation. As a result, many schools stalled integration for as long as possible.

Arkansas was one of the southern states that stalled integration.

Washington, D.C.

ARKANSAS

Little Rock

Little Rock, Arkansas

In 1955, in Little Rock, Arkansas, the school board started a plan for integration in Little Rock Central High School. The plan called for desegregation to begin in the fall of 1957 and to slowly move through the lower grades over the next six years. Students would be allowed to move from any school where their race was in the minority.

Daisy Bates (back row, second from the right) and the Little Rock Nine students.

Daisy Bates

Daisy Bates was a key figure in school integration in Arkansas. She was a member of the NAACP and in 1952 became president of the Arkansas section of the organization. It was Daisy's job to find African American students to integrate Little Rock Central High School.

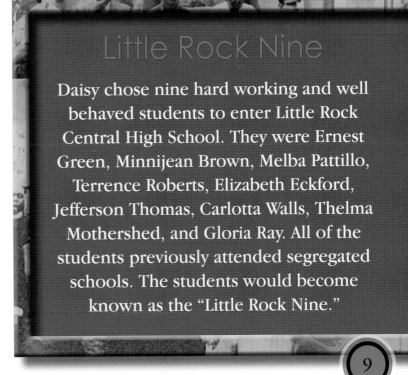

Little Rock Nine

Daisy chose nine hard working and well behaved students to enter Little Rock Central High School. They were Ernest Green, Minnijean Brown, Melba Pattillo, Terrence Roberts, Elizabeth Eckford, Jefferson Thomas, Carlotta Walls, Thelma Mothershed, and Gloria Ray. All of the students previously attended segregated schools. The students would become known as the "Little Rock Nine."

Integration

It soon became clear that integration in Little Rock was not going to be easy. Many white Americans in the state were not in favor of desegregation. Orval Faubus, the governor of Arkansas at the time, recognized this.

Losing Votes

During his campaign to be governor, Faubus promised to spend money on schools and education in the state.

> "There is evidence of disorder and threats of disorder which could have but one inevitable result, that is violence, which can lead to injury and harm to persons or property."
>
> Orval Faubus, speaking about his reasons for stopping integration at Little Rock Central High School.

Orval Faubus thought that integration at Little Rock Central High School would make him unpopular with voters.

The National Guard were ordered to other schools, too. Here, they stand guard at the Clinton High School in Tennessee.

In the first few months after he became governor, Faubus even put an end to some segregation in Arkansas by desegregating buses and public transport. However, Faubus knew that the planned integration at Little Rock Central High School was not popular with many white Americans. He was worried that he would lose votes, and his position as governor, if he let Little Rock Central High School integrate. He decided to take action.

Blocking the Nine Students

On September 2, 1957, Faubus called in the National Guard to stop the nine students selected by Daisy Bates from entering Little Rock Central High School. Faubus declared the school off-limits to African Americans. Faubus had also previously declared Horace Mann, the African American high school, off-limits to white Americans.

We Will Integrate!

The NAACP decided that they would continue with their integration plans, despite the declaration by Orval Faubus that Little Rock Central High School would not desegregate. On September 4, 1957, Daisy Bates arranged for the nine students chosen for integration to meet a few blocks from Little Rock Central High, and walk to the school together.

Chased Away

Only seven of the nine students managed to meet Daisy on September 4, the first day of school. The eighth student, Melba Pattillo, tried to meet with the group, but was chased away by a crowd of angry white Americans. Elizabeth Eckford never received Daisy's message.

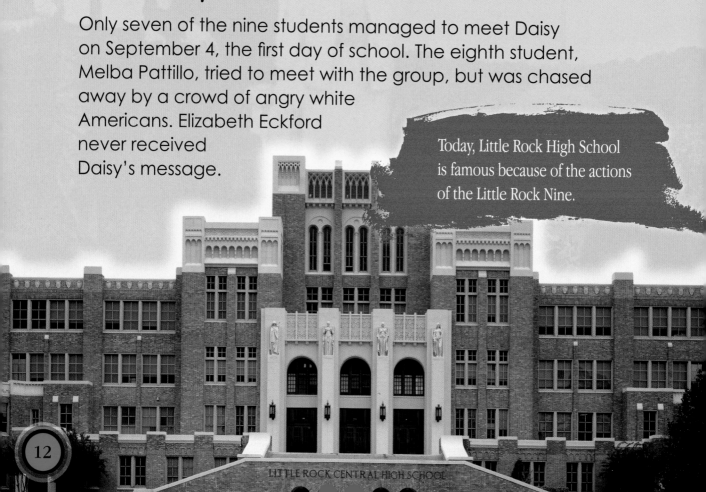

Today, Little Rock High School is famous because of the actions of the Little Rock Nine.

LITTLE ROCK CENTRAL HIGH SCHOOL

Elizabeth Eckford was shouted at by angry white Americans.

Threats and Name-Calling

After they had met, the group of seven students and Daisy set off for Little Rock Central High School, accompanied by four ministers. As they turned a street corner on their route to school, they were confronted by an angry crowd, who shouted names and waved banners at the students, Daisy, and the ministers.

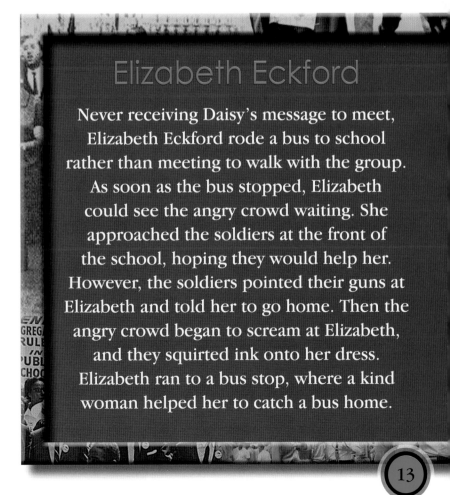

Elizabeth Eckford

Never receiving Daisy's message to meet, Elizabeth Eckford rode a bus to school rather than meeting to walk with the group. As soon as the bus stopped, Elizabeth could see the angry crowd waiting. She approached the soldiers at the front of the school, hoping they would help her. However, the soldiers pointed their guns at Elizabeth and told her to go home. Then the angry crowd began to scream at Elizabeth, and they squirted ink onto her dress. Elizabeth ran to a bus stop, where a kind woman helped her to catch a bus home.

A Year of Torment

Even once the nine students managed to attend Little Rock Central High daily, the difficulties of school life continued. In November, the soldiers withdrew and the students faced school without guard. Most white American students at Little Rock Central High were kind to the African American students, but a few were very cruel.

Backing the Students

Daisy Bates remained close to all of the students during their difficult time at Little Rock Central High. She was there to offer support and advice whenever the students needed it. The students' parents also played an important role. The parents sent President Eisenhower a telegram thanking him for his involvement and for protecting their children, and urging him to accept school integration.

Lunchtime

The African American students dreaded lunchtime. They had to enter a hall full of white American students, some of whom clearly did not want African American students at their school.

Fighting Back

The nine students had grown used to being called names, pushed, and kicked. However, they were not prepared to have food thrown over them. Minnijean Brown decided she just couldn't take it any more. Minnijean dropped her lunch tray on two white boys, and when a white girl hit her, she called her a name.

"I just can't take everything they throw at me without fighting back."
Minnijean Brown.

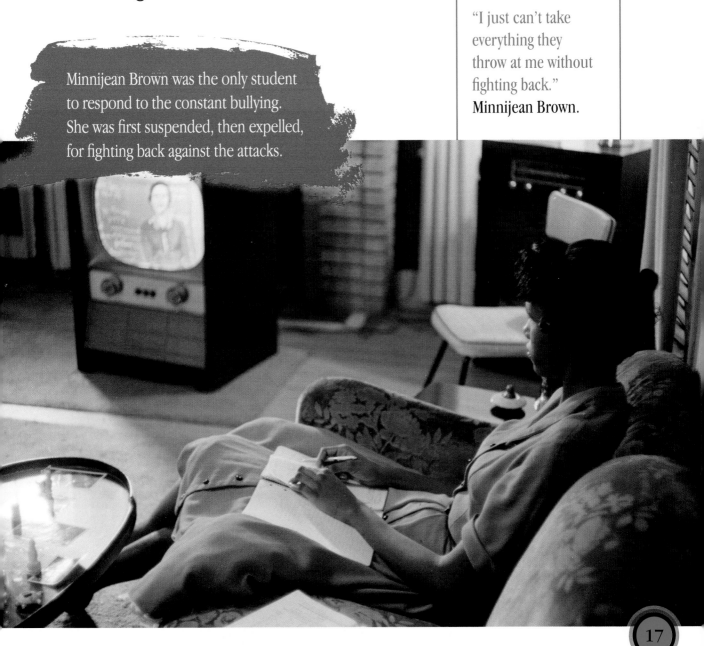

Minnijean Brown was the only student to respond to the constant bullying. She was first suspended, then expelled, for fighting back against the attacks.

Graduation at Last

The eight African American students who remained at Little Rock Central High after the expulsion of Minnijean Brown continued to face verbal and physical bullying. Yet, they also continued to attend the school until the end of the year.

> "It's been an interesting year. I've had a course in human relations firsthand."
> **Ernest Green.**

First African American Graduate

On May 27, 1958, Ernest Green became the first African American to graduate from Little Rock Central High School. Without the support of the other eight African American students, this would not have been possible. All nine students had remained strong in the face of armed troops and had helped to bring about desegregation in Little Rock.

Ernest Green was the first of the Little Rock Nine students to graduate.

The Little Rock Nine met the New York City mayor, Robert Wagner, who congratulated them on integrating the school.

School Closure

The following year, in an attempt to stop desegregation in Arkansas schools, Governor Faubus closed all high schools in Little Rock. This meant that students had to study at home or attend schools in other cities. However, the school board reopened the schools in 1959. Jefferson Thomas and Carlotta Walls returned to Little Rock Central High that year and followed in Ernest's footsteps by graduating in 1960.

The Spingarn Medal

In 1958, Daisy Bates and the Little Rock Nine were given the NAACP's highest honor, the Spingarn Medal. This medal is awarded for outstanding achievements of African Americans.

The Little Rock Example

The events at Little Rock Central High School had caught the nation's attention. All over the country, school integration was taking place, and a number of schools in different states desegregated peacefully. However, in some areas, resistance to school desegregation ended in violence.

> "The whole nation took one giant step forward."
> **Melba Pattillo.**

Protests and Violence

Clinton High School in Tennessee was one of the first public schools to integrate. Twelve African American students registered to attend the school, and on August 27, 1956, ten of them walked to the Green McAdoo School without any problems. By the next day, however, the students received threats of violence from a waiting angry crowd. Protesters against integration smashed windows, damaged cars, and threatened to blow up buildings. The National Guard were called in to keep order and remained outside the school for two weeks. In December, a minister was badly beaten after walking the twelve students to school.

A statue of the students who successfully integrated one of the first high schools in the South, Clinton High School, stands at the entrance to the Green McAdoo Cultural Center in Clinton, Tennessee.

Integration in Alabama

In September 1963, schools in Tuskegee, Birmingham, Mobile, and Huntsville were due to be integrated. However, Alabama's governor, George Wallace, did not agree with the plans. Wallace sent soldiers to a high school in Tuskegee to stop 13 African American students attending. The soldiers turned away all pupils and teachers trying to enter the school. Eventually, President Kennedy sent in the National Guard to help desegregate the school.

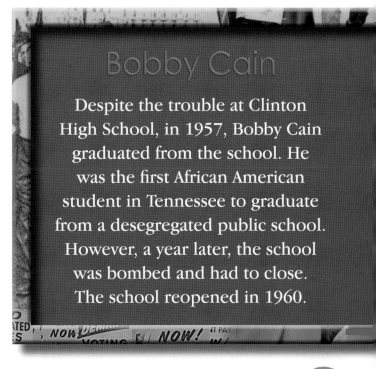

Bobby Cain

Despite the trouble at Clinton High School, in 1957, Bobby Cain graduated from the school. He was the first African American student in Tennessee to graduate from a desegregated public school. However, a year later, the school was bombed and had to close. The school reopened in 1960.

21

After Little Rock

Despite the integration at Little Rock Central High, some people were still against school integration. Two years after the students had first entered the school in 1959, a protest about integration took place at the Arkansas State Capitol building.

Rally at State Capitol

Hundreds of protesters marched to the State Capitol building, the main government building in Little Rock, to protest about the integration of the school. Some carried banners that read "Stop the race mixing."

Angry crowds gathered outside the Arkansas State Capitol building to protest about school integration.

Arrests and Protests

Many of the protesters marched on to Little Rock Central High School, where they faced police and fire crews who broke up the crowd. Twenty-one people were arrested.

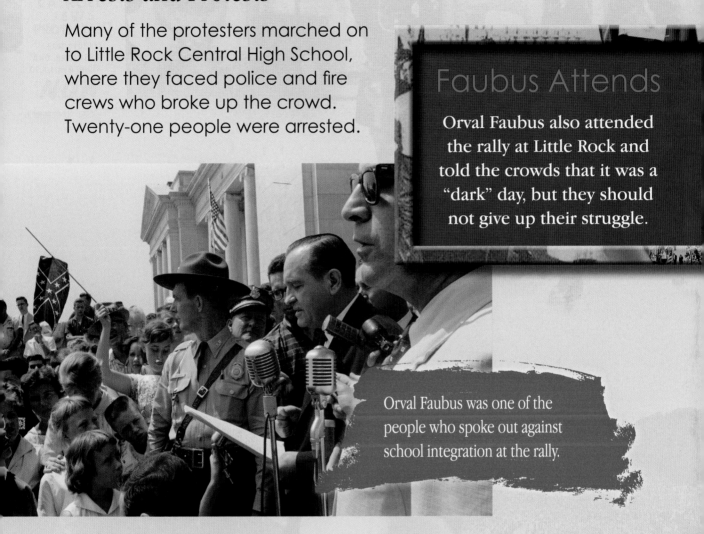

Faubus Attends

Orval Faubus also attended the rally at Little Rock and told the crowds that it was a "dark" day, but they should not give up their struggle.

Orval Faubus was one of the people who spoke out against school integration at the rally.

Great Achievers

Several of the Little Rock Nine went on to achieve great things. Elizabeth Eckford joined the army, and Ernest Green served as assistant secretary of the federal Department of Labor, under President Jimmy Carter. Minnijean Brown worked as deputy assistant secretary for workforce diversity, under President Bill Clinton. Melba Pattillo worked as a reporter for the NBC television channel. Other members of the Little Rock Nine achieved great success, too.

The Civil Rights Movement

Little Rock Central High was an important part of American school integration, but it was also part of a wider movement across the United States. This was a protest in which African Americans demanded equal rights in all areas of life.

Montgomery Buses

In 1955, two years before the integration at Little Rock, an African American woman named Rosa Parks made a stand against segregation on public transport. In Montgomery, Alabama, where she lived, Rosa refused to give up her seat on a bus for a white passenger. She was arrested and taken to jail. A protest was then arranged, in which thousands of African Americans stopped using Montgomery's buses for more than a year. Eventually, the US Supreme Court ruled that all buses in Montgomery would be desegregated.

Rosa Parks continued to be an active civil rights campaigner long after the Montgomery Bus Boycott.

An exhibit retelling the sit-in at the Woolworth's department store in Greensboro is on display at the National Civil Rights Museum in Memphis, Tennessee.

Silent Sit-Ins

Protests against segregation in restaurants were also taking place at the same time as school desegregation. When four African American students took seats at a "whites only" lunch counter in Woolworth's store in Greensboro, North Carolina, they were refused service. However, the students continued to sit peacefully at the counter. These "sit-ins," as they became known, soon spread to lunch counters elsewhere across the United States. Stores eventually began to desegregate their lunch counters and serve African American customers.

The March on Washington for Jobs and Freedom

In 1963, after months of planning by civil rights organizations, hundreds of thousands of Americans descended upon Washington, D.C. in a peaceful protest. The aim of the march was to protest for equal rights in jobs and freedom for all Americans, African Americans and white Americans alike.

The Civil Rights Act

The 1963 March on Washington for Jobs and Freedom won the attention of the nation and the president himself. As part of John F. Kennedy's election campaign, he proposed a Civil Rights Act and won more than 70 percent of the African American vote in his 1963 election. Kennedy's Civil Rights bill was in progress when the president was assassinated in 1963.

Hundreds of thousands of peaceful protesters, both white and African American, took part in The March on Washington for Jobs and Freedom.

The Civil Rights Act

After Kennedy's death, President Lyndon B. Johnson took up the fight to make Kennedy's bill law. Eventually, in 1964, the Civil Rights Act was signed, making racial discrimination in public places, such as theaters, restaurants, and hotels, illegal. It also meant that employers had to provide equal employment opportunities for African Americans.

Huge Change

The Voting Rights Act was signed just one year after the Civil Rights Act was passed. This law meant that any American citizen could vote. By the end of 1966, just under 50 percent of African Americans were registered to vote in just four of the 13 southern states. This meant that far more African Americans were elected into public office. This Voting Rights Act gave the civil rights movement a huge boost and paved the way for enormous change.

In 2007, President Bill Clinton spoke at the 50th anniversary of the integration at Little Rock Central High School.

A Lasting Legacy

In 2008, an African American was elected as President of the United States of America. That would have been unthinkable were it not for the actions of nine Arkansas students who decided they had the right to apply to, and attend, Little Rock Central High School. The Little Rock Nine knew they would face people who didn't want them there, and even violence, but they bravely continued with their plans. Without them, the United States as we know it today might be very different.

"I try to get young people today to understand that it's a violent world, but nonviolent activism is the most powerful force."
Minnijean Brown.

A statue of the Little Rock Nine stands in the grounds of the Arkansas State Capitol building in Little Rock.

In 2009, Barack Obama invited the Little Rock Nine to attend his inauguration ceremony.

The Right to Learn

The Little Rock Nine were part of a great, sweeping movement that changed the lives of African Americans forever. Were it not for the bravery of those nine students, African American children in the United States today would not have the right to go to school with white American children or the right to an equal education. Thanks to the Little Rock Nine, all American children, and their children to come, have the right to an education, whatever their color.

The Little Rock Nine Foundation

The Little Rock Nine also set up and run the Little Rock Nine Foundation. It is a support group that provides teaching and financial support to enable students to reach their education goals.

Glossary

assassinated (uh-SA-suh-nayt-ed) Murdered for political reasons.

campaign (kam-PAYN) A series of planned actions to reach a particular goal.

desegregated (dee-SEH-gruh-gayt-ed) To stop the use of separate schools and facilities for people of different races.

election (ee-LEK-shun) The process of choosing a person to serve in government by voting.

equal rights (ee-KWUL RYTS) The same rights for all people.

escorted (es-KORT-ed) Traveled with someone (or a group of people) to protect them.

expulsion (ek-SPUL-shun) Forced to leave school.

governor (GUH-vur-nur) A person who leads a state.

graduate (GRA-juh-wayt) To finish studies at high school or college.

human relations (HYOO-mun rih-LAY-shunz) The way that people communicate or behave with each other.

integration (in-tuh-GRAY-shun) To bring together, to mix.

Jim Crow laws (JIM KROH LOZ) Laws in the southern states that kept African Americans separate from white Americans.

minister (MIH-nuh-stur) Someone who can perform or help at religious services.

minority (my-NOR-ih-tee) A group of people who are different from the larger population in some way.

National Guard (NASH-nul GARD) A US military force maintained by each state, but subject to the call of another state or the federal government.

protesters (PROH-test-urz) A group of people who take action against something they believe is wrong.

race (RAYS) A section of the human population that share certain common physical qualities.

racial discrimination (RAY-shul dis-krih-muh-NAY-shun) Treating people of a certain race differently.

secretary (SEK-ruh-ter-ee) An official who is the head of a government department.

segregation (seh-gruh-GAY-shun) A system to keep white Americans and African Americans apart.

Supreme Court (suh-PREEM KORT) The highest court in the United States.

telegram (TEL-uh-gram) A message sent over wires, using code that is then printed and delivered by hand.

verbal (VER-bul) Spoken words.

vote (VOHT) A person's choice in a group decision; people vote for who they want in government.

Further Reading

Jeffrey, Gary. *The Little Rock Nine and the Fight for Equal Rights*. A Graphic History of the Civil Rights Movement. New York: Gareth Stevens Learning Library, 2012.

Skog, Jason. *The Civil Rights Act of 1964*. We the People: Modern America. Mankato, MN: Compass Point Books, 2007.

Zeiger, Jennifer. *The Civil Rights Movement*. Cornerstones of Freedom. Danbury, CT: Children's Press, 2011.

Websites

Due to the changing nature of Internet links, PowerKids Press has developed an online list of websites related to the subject of this book. This site is updated regularly. Please use this link to access the list:
www.powerkidslinks.com/wso/little/

Index